THE ESS
TO 100% GUILT-FREE
SELF-CARE

*Get Your Time +
Energy Back to
Create the World
You Want to Live In*

TAMI HACKBARTH

MariTess

THE ESSENTIAL GUIDE TO 100% GUILT-FREE SELF-CARE

Author Name
Tami Hackbarth

Publisher Name
MariTess Press

Contact Information
www.tamihackbarth.com | tami@tamihackbarth.com

The Essential Guide to 100% Guilt-Free Self-Care
Tami Hackbarth —1st ed.

ISBN: 979-8-9871629-0-3

Dedication

To my ATeam: Thank you for supporting me along the way. What a relief to be loved because I am me.

To my daughter: You are my best girl. I am the luckiest mama. Thank you for being you.

CONTENTS

Introduction

Self-care isn't selfish.
Self-care is the fuel for your
life.

I am not talking about manicures, pedicures, and massages.

Don't get me wrong, those are lovely.

The self-care I am talking about in this book is the kind that might not sound fun or be particularly enjoyable but done often enough, it will add to your long-term well-being.

Practicing self-care is the difference between having the bandwidth and energy to create the world you want to live in or not.

So why don't more people prioritize their own care?

It is a story as old as time; women are exhausted because a majority of care tasks and household labor fall on their shoulders at home and at work.

Some of the daily drudgery tasks that fall disproportionately on women:

- feeding people

- clothing people

- cleaning spaces

- inventory management

- making sure household supplies and systems are in good condition

- managing healthcare

- maintaining relationships

- planning vacations and parties

- buying gifts

- knowing the school schedules

- being the person school calls first when a child is sick

Most women think if they just get more organized or stay on top of everything and everyone, then they will have time for themselves.

If we think about doing less or asking for help, many women believe we are lazy and selfish.

Sometimes people even say that out loud, and often we say these things to ourselves.

If we think about doing less or asking for help, many women believe we are lazy and selfish.

Sometimes people even say that out loud, and often we say these things to ourselves.

I haven't ever met a lazy woman.

I have only met exhausted and overworked women because of the mental load they are expected to carry on their own and the endless care tasks that fall to them by default.

We can tell a different story than the one that was told to us.

We can show our children, friends, and family that we all deserve to get our needs met.

We can show the world that we matter by showing ourselves we matter.

WE CAN CHANGE HOW OUR STORY ENDS.

Don't get me wrong; this isn't a strictly personal issue.

There are systemic issues that get in the way as well:

- the lack of quality and affordable child care and early childhood education

- access to the full spectrum of reproductive health services

- the access to equitable education

- paid family leave

- paid sick leave

- a liveable minimum wage

- universal basic income

- access to quality mental health services

...to name a few.

All of this disproportionately affects women of color more because of systematic racism and LGBTQ+ folks because of homophobia and gender bias.

We have so much work to do, and it is damn near impossible to change these structural issues without the energy and bandwidth.

This is our chance to change this dynamic.

We can create more energy and bandwidth with strategic self-care practices.

We can reject the unequal and unfair unpaid labor of our households, and we can work to change the laws that keep us exhausted.

We can work to make our significant relationships have a more equitable division of labor and we can also demand better social support from our government.

Our significant others and children can do more household labor, and we can advocate for every family to have their basic needs met.

The more that the work of life is redistributed, the more time we have to care for ourselves and the better chance we have at changing this dynamic for future generations.

How we spend that time is up to us, but my vote is for pouring into ourselves, so we have more energy and bandwidth to create the world we want to live in.

We can do both, I promise!

When we prioritize our own care, we show the people around us that we matter too.

We model new ways of being in the world to those around us and give everyone else permission to care for themselves in the ways that matter most.

It is from that place that we have the energy to do the work of being the best version of ourselves who can help create a more fair, equitable, and just world.

Don't Believe Everything You Think

A belief is a repeated thought.

Just because you think something over and over again doesn't make it true.

We can change what we believe by changing the stories we tell ourselves.

Below is a list of common beliefs about self-care.

Not every one of these beliefs will be yours.

- Which of the following beliefs do you identify with?

- Where did you first hear them?

- Who else that you know believes them?

- Who benefits from you continuing to believe?

- What in your life would change if you changed your beliefs?

What Gets In Your Way?

Believing self-care is too expensive.

> This book covers the basics of 100% Guilt-Free Self-Care. This is exactly what I do with my clients - all for the cost of this book.

> By the end of this book, you will know your current state of self-care and have a plan for guilt-free self-care actions. All you need to do is execute.

Believing self-care is too time-consuming.

> Yes, taking care of yourself does take time. Most likely, it takes less time than you think it does.

> Isn't feeling the way you want to feel in your life worth investing some of your time?

Believing self-care takes away from your family.

> So much self-care can be done as a family. You can set a bedtime for yourself along with your kids.

> You can challenge your kids to a game of kickball or soccer.

You can plan and cook produce-forward recipes together.

You can have family quiet time on weekend afternoons. You can have dance parties in your kitchen.

You set the emotional tone in your family, so you can speak kindly to yourself and show your kids how to have a growth mindset which is the belief that we have the power to learn and change with effort.

Believing you have to do it all or it doesn't count.

If you take one thing from this book, it is small actions matter. The 20-minute walk you take at lunch is better than the 3-mile run you never have time for.

The 3 minutes of meditation are better than the zero minutes you do because you can never seem to find the time for the 30 minutes every single day.

The one restorative yoga pose does more to calm your nervous system than the 60 minutes of power yoga class you rush to attend.

The tiniest bit of compassion will allow you to show up more for yourself and others than the never-ending self-criticism will.

Believing that change isn't possible.

I know it feels that way sometimes. Especially when we are faced with seismic changes.

The best way I know how to get started when things feel impossible is to look for the next small step, the 1% difference.

Making the steps so small you can get started without falling into overwhelm is key.

One baby step at a time.

Believing you will have time later.

Is this a good time to tell you that later is not guaranteed and that things can change in an instant?

You or your loved one can get into an accident, lose a job, or have to take care of a sick or dying relative or friend.

If you are running on fumes before a crisis hits, how will you handle this extra challenge?

Sooner than you know it, you will be caring for an elderly person - yourself or someone else.

Think of your current self-care as compound interest in your future senior self.

Believing that you will be different tomorrow than you are now.

Later is not a magical place where everything falls into place.

We continue to be who we are today unless we make active changes.

It is up to you to carve out time today to prioritize your mental and physical health and well-being before later catches up to you.

Sooner than you realize, you will be a senior citizen yourself.

Strong, healthy, mobile seniors are created in midlife and before.

Carve out time now to build a reserve of energy for a crisis and get a head start on tending to your future self.

Believing you are alone.

Not having support makes everything in life so much harder.

Asking friends to work on their self-care with you while you work on yours will help everyone feel less alone.

Taking a walk with a friend builds connection, accountability, and good habits.

Joining a community of like-minded people with similar goals helps build the support you need.

This is the purpose of my Deferred Maintenance community.

We are better together.

Believing you will fail.

You've tried so many things in the past and didn't follow through and quit.

Girl, same! It is okay to start over again.

You are never starting from scratch because you have previous experience to guide you through obstacles and to make different choices this time.

Quit quitting on yourself. Just start again.

Believing you are a hot mess.

I know it feels like everyone but you has their life together.

But I am here to tell you we are all in this together.

We are all imperfect humans.

We are all figuring it out as we go.

Everyone has stuff they are working on and in various stages of figuring things out for the moment.

Even people who seem like their life is perfect, it doesn't feel that way to them.

Stop comparing your insides to everyone else's outsides.

Believing you are high maintenance.

Don't we all wish life was effortless and easy? I sure do!

But what I've learned in my over half-century of living is that if you want things to last, you gotta take care of them.

Think about your car or cashmere sweater - doing the bare minimum will leave them looking and working ok, but spending a little more time and effort will allow them to last a really long time and look good while doing it.

Believing you shouldn't have needs.

All living things have needs. All human beings have needs. You are human, so you have needs.

Having them doesn't make you high maintenance.

Needs don't make you broken or fussy - they make you human.

The more our needs are met consistently, the better we feel in each moment and the more energy we have to show up and do the work of creating the world we want to live in.

Believing there is something wrong with me because I am not happy even when I get to do stuff for myself.

You aren't a bottomless pit of need.

Most likely, your needs have been on the back burner, and it's been a really long time since you have tended to your needs.

You didn't get where you are today overnight, and most likely, it will take time to fill that care gap.

Please be patient and gentle with yourself.

Did you know?

Turns out there are different kinds of happiness.

One that leaves us wanting more, and the other builds a deep sense of contentment.

Hedonistic happiness is a quick hit of pleasure.

This is the kind we read about in magazines and see on social media: shopping, happy hour - cocktails with co-workers, a weekend away with friends in Las Vegas dancing the night away. Fun in the moment, but doesn't get into the deeper longing for a meaningful life.

The other kind of happiness - Eudaimonic happiness - comes from the deep satisfaction about doing the things that will create a meaningful life, even if they aren't particularly pleasant while you are doing them.

Some examples are:

- meditation

- strength training

- learning and practicing nonviolent communication

- flossing your teeth

- working with a therapist to resolve some long-standing issues.

Not sexy or fun at the moment, but your future self will thank you.

Our lives have room for both kinds of happiness.

100% Guilt-Free Self-Care in this book is meant to foster long-term well-being and what I refer to as taking care of our future senior citizen selves.

How different would the world be if each of us has all our needs met?

A World of Difference - My Story

Growing up in the 70s, I didn't learn anything about self-care. It wasn't something anyone talked about.

I didn't even really observe anyone practicing it. I didn't know anyone who worked out.

I didn't know anyone took time for themselves to meditate or recharge.

Therapy was something people whispered about, if it was mentioned at all, and no one talked positively about boundaries.

The people I knew went to work, did housework and maybe went on a regional trip with their family once a year for their vacation.

Eventually, Jazzercise, Jane Fonda, and jogging became mainstream in the 80s.

I loved going to aerobics classes with my stepmom wearing tights and leotards.

The overall message behind the fitness craze was all about appearance and staying skinny.

Special K for breakfast, TAB with lunch, and cigarettes as a diet tool.

It was a different time!

It wasn't until I was in therapy in the early 90s that I was taught to do some stuff at home to help me feel better between sessions.

It was there I first heard about meditation, taking a walk outside to boost mental health, focusing on getting good sleep, and cutting back on alcohol and smoking.

This is where I first learned the difference between knowing something and doing something.

I knew what to do; I didn't know how to make it part of my everyday life.

I didn't yet know how to break bad habits and create healthy ones.

I wasn't even sure change was really possible for me.

Starting my career in politics in the late 90s, I was immediately caught up in the culture of long work hours, frequent happy hours, and eating whatever was around.

My skin was broken out; I constantly had a stomach ache, and I had trouble sleeping.

I felt awful, and I struggled to make changes because no one I knew was practicing good self-care.

I felt alone and deeply flawed.

I was raised with the idea that we were dealt certain cards in our lifetime, and we were stuck with those cards.

That either you were a happy person or not. That you were a healthy person or not.

Eventually, I changed careers and studied to be a teacher.

There is an undercurrent in the teaching profession that you should give to others until you drop.

In fact, an acupuncturist told me I was going to drop dead in my classroom if I didn't deal with my stress.

My internal response was, "rude."

I didn't want to hear the truth that I needed to make changes in my life.

I just want him to help clear up my skin. Preferably without an effort or changes on my part.

This wasn't the first time I heard stress was a killer, but I didn't know how to create new habits or if that was even possible.

Up until that point, I felt like I was really good at creating bad habits, and not sure how to stop those and certainly didn't have any idea how to create good ones to replace them.

I knew things had to change when midyear, my principal asked me if I was happy being a teacher.

Never in a million years did I think anyone would ever ask me that because I felt teaching was my calling.

I kicked ass in the classroom as a teacher.

But he wanted to know if I'd be happy doing something else because he didn't see a single ounce of joy on my face.

My response was to burst into ugly tears.

The truth of it is I wasn't happy.

I couldn't see myself doing anything else, but I couldn't find the joy.

In the past, when I felt this way, I quit my job and tried somewhere else.

But this time, I wanted to stay. I wanted to figure it out.

Something needed to change, and that was me.

The first thing I did was put some pretty firm time boundaries around my work.

I arrived on time and left on time - no more 12-hour work days for me.

I had a research project to do. I needed to figure out how to be happier and healthier.

Instead of spending every free moment of my life working, I started going to yoga classes.

I started cooking dinner and making sure I had good leftovers for lunch.

I started making plans with friends for fun. I started reading a ton of books about happiness, productivity, and designing your life.

Soon I found The Happiness Project by Gretchen Rubin. In the book, Rubin described her plan to become a little happier by taking on small habit changes each month in different aspects of her life.

This created a lightbulb moment for me: small daily actions could have a huge impact.

An Obsession With Small Things

I became obsessed with the idea of changing small things in your life to make big changes over time.

I became obsessed with being curious about what would help me become happier.

"What I do matters" is the most life-changing discovery of my life!

It was then that I decided I would try to lead my life as someone who is doing experiments.

I put on my (metaphorical) scientist hat and got out my clipboard to take notes to see what would happen when I prioritize my own self-care.

I learned quickly that trying to change everything at once was a recipe for disaster.

So eventually, I decided to focus on the basics one category at a time.

- What in my life would change if I was to sleep well?

- How would I need to change my habits to consistently get good sleep?

- What gets in the way of my sleep?

- What small tweaks could I make over time to get even better sleep?

- What in my life would change if I was to eat well?

What did I even mean by that? Who decides?

What foods help my body feel good, and what leaves me feeling not so good?

How do I make sure I always have what I need in the kitchen? When and where do I shop? What recipes will I use?

What in my life would change if I exercised consistently?

Like most people, I knew that exercise would benefit me by reducing my stress and helping me sleep.

Up until that point though I worked out because I wanted my body to look a certain way.

Getting curious about the way that movement affected my mental health created a whole new way of looking at this form of self-care.

What in my life would change if I carved out a few minutes a day to get quiet and meditate?

I had experience with meditation in yoga classes before. I had felt that fleeting sense of peace at the end of class.

Would it be possible to experience more peace and less negative chatter in my head on my own?

What would happen if I stopped taking things personally?

Instead of black-or-white thinking - what if I got curious about a more nuanced, greyscale world?

What if right or wrong, good or bad, I could lean into less judgment and more curiosity?

How would I talk about myself through that lens? How different would the world look through that lens?

Within days I could see the difference in my mood. I was all in.

I spent the remainder of that school year experimenting and taking notes.

Final result: When I felt better, everything was better.

My students did better socially and academically. I got along better with my spouse.

I felt more energetic and hopeful. I was less overwhelmed even during busy times.

I felt like I had the bandwidth to show up well in my life.

Over the next decade, I became a mom, and I decided to take what I learned - and bring it to other teachers and parents.

In my work over the last decade, my clients have all had great success changing how they feel in their lives.

They change what they believe is possible. They create new healthy habits.

They create a new community of supporters.

They create new ways of being in the world. They change their family dynamics.

They change how their children see them.

In short, they are changing the world.

Mindset Matters

The biggest factor in whether we make a change in our lives is if we believe change is possible.

- Does what we do matter or not? In other words, do we have a growth mindset or a fixed mindset?

- Do you believe that you are able to change your habits and future if you know what to do?

- Do you believe that you're able to change your habits and future if you know what to do and how to do it?

- Do you believe that you're able to change your habits and future if you know what to do, how to do it, and have accountability and support?

- Do you believe you were born the way you are and what you do doesn't matter much?

Please yourself on a scale of 1-10: how committed are you to making changes in your life in order to get more time and energy?

If you are in the 7-10 range, you are ready to take imperfect action. I can't wait to dive in with you!

If you are in the 4-6 range, you are thinking about taking action and may need some convincing why this is important and why now is the time.

If you are in the 1-3 range, I am sending you hugs and hope that you are inspired to start believing that what you do matters in how you feel in your life.

No matter where you are currently, being kind to yourself will help get you where you want to be.

Knowing that everyone has their own struggles can help remind us that we aren't alone in ours.

Keeping those two things in mind while you make changes in your life will help you move forward into a more energetic space.

How to Use This Book

This guide is meant to give you a place to start when you aren't sure what to do, what to do next, or what to do when what you have been doing isn't helping you.

It is not meant to make you feel like you are behind or that you suck at being a grown-up.

Or think of this as another list of things you have to do perfectly or feel bad about not doing.

This isn't meant for you to beat yourself up about your current level of self-care or the season of your life.

My advice is to start with the body essentials section because it is hard to do anything when your basic human needs aren't being met.

It is these unsexy daily habits and routines that help us get started and allow us to keep doing what needs to be done to feel the way we want to feel.

Getting Comfortable With Discomfort

Deciding to change how you spend your time and shifting your priorities will inevitably lead to discomfort.

You might feel uncomfortable because you haven't focused your attention on yourself in a long time.

You may also really hate disappointing others, especially those you love the most.

Others in your life might resist your changes and wish you could go back to the way you were.

Change is hard for everyone and if you are able to sit with the discomfort you will get to the other side of it.

Change takes time and courage. You've got this.

The 100% Guilt-Free
Self-Care Framework

The framework in this book addresses four major aspects of well-being: the physical body, our mental health, the relationship with ourselves and others and our place in the bigger community.

What is your current state of well-being and your physical body?

> Please record your current quality and quantity of sleep that you are getting over the course of a week. No judgment, just collect data.

Next, evaluate your current diet.

> What are you eating that makes you feel good? What are you eating that makes you feel not so great?

Next, evaluate your current exercise routine.

> How are you moving your body? What is the frequency that you're exercising? What is the intensity? What level of enjoyment are you getting from the movement practices in your life?

Finally, evaluate the quiet space in your life.

What's the current state of your meditation practice? are you sitting for a quiet contemplation or praying a few minutes a day? Are you taking walks outside without the distraction of your phone?

What kind of space do you have in your schedule? What kind of downtime do you have each day or week?

Do the same kind of evaluation for your mental health, your relationship with yourself and your relationship with others.

Be sure to also evaluate the current state of your spiritual life and your place is a bigger community in the world.

Reminder: you are looking for data, patterns and a baseline. Leave the judgment out of your investigation.

The **100% Guilt-Free Self-Care Assessment** will give you some information on where your self-care is now and what needs more attention.

The **100% Guilt-Free Self-Care Planner** will help you decide where to focus your efforts.

Both tools and videos can be found at www.tamihackbarth.com/bookresources.

I

The Body Essentials

Non-Negotiable Human Maintenance

THE UNSEXY TRUTH ABOUT SLEEP

When was the last time you felt truly rested? We live in a 24-hour news cycle culture.

We're expected to be ready and available at all times.

We live with the cultural belief that exhaustion is a status symbol and that being busy means you are important.

Sacrificing sleep in the name of productivity is common.

Pair this with the belief that everything must be completed before we rest, and there are a lot of exhausted people out there.

This is especially true for women because so much of the day-to-day never-ending care tasks.

Resting when you are tired and getting regular sleep isn't a sign of weakness, but rather the fuel for your whole life.

According to Harvard Medical School, the lack of sleep affects your memory, mood, motivation, judgment, and perception of events.

Not getting enough sleep can also increase errors at work, decrease productivity and cause accidents.

It can even make you gain weight if you are sleeping less than seven hours a night.

When it comes down to it, sleep is the foundation for 100% Guilt-Free Self-Care.

Making small changes to what you do during the day can help you be ready for sleep at bedtime.

What are some secrets to getting more sleep?

- Prioritizing rest over getting everything done. Letting go of the idea that you must earn rest will help too.

Good sleep really starts hours and hours before bedtime. In order to be tired and ready for bed, we need to:

- Limit caffeine, alcohol, and nicotine (stimulants and depressants) and stressful events before bedtime.

- Get your bedroom ready for sleep: cool, dark, and quiet.

- Practice a pre-bed routine: turn off screens an hour before bed, take a bath, read a book, meditate, and practice relaxation techniques.

100% GUILT-FREE SELF-CARE ACTION:

Get more sleep tonight (and every night). It may take a while to get to a place where you feel rested.

Most likely, you've been tired for a long time. Keep at it. Sleep will change your life!

SOME QUESTIONS TO WRITE ABOUT IN YOUR SELF-CARE JOURNAL.

How much sleep do you need in order to feel rested?

When was the last time you were truly well-rested?

What are some things that keep you from sleeping?

Are you revenge procrastinating because after your family goes to sleep is the only time you have to yourself?

What are some of the things that you believe about people who get enough sleep?

Fuel Your Body With Food

We all have to eat to fuel our bodies.

Often people forget that eating is something that we will do at least 21 times a week in order to keep ourselves going.

There is food advice coming at us from all directions.

One thing most of us are most likely missing is enough fruit and vegetables.

According to the Center for Disease Control, eating more fruits and vegetables:

- Adds nutrients to your diet that your body needs.

- Reduces the risk of heart disease, stroke, and some cancers.

- Helps manage body weight when eaten instead of other non-fruit and veggie foods.

The CDC says we need to eat one and a half to two fruit AND two to three cups of vegetables a day.

It sounds like a lot, but I challenge you to see for yourself. You can find photos online or get out your produce and measuring cups and start chopping.

What are some secrets for getting more fruits and veggies in your body?

- Make them visible. Keep a bowl on the kitchen counter or on your desk at work.

- Create a rainbow in the refrigerator. Take your fruit and vegetables out of the drawers, prep them, and display them on the top shelf in clear glass jars at eye level. This is using planning and preparation to take care of your future self.

- Aim to have either a fruit or vegetable at every meal every day.

100% GUILT-FREE SELF-CARE ACTION:

Plan and prepare fruit and vegetables so you can eat them today.

Bring produce to work or school with you, so you have what you need for the day.

Repeat.

SOME FOOD-RELATED QUESTIONS TO WRITE ABOUT IN YOUR SELF-CARE JOURNAL.

Which fruits and vegetables do you already love?

What food rules did you have growing up, and how did they make you feel?

What are some food rules you follow now, and how do they make you feel?

Exercise is a Four Letter Word

Seriously, everyone I talk to has a story about exercise.

Either it is too hard, it takes too much time, it hurts when they do it, it is too expensive, it is too boring, and no one thinks what they are doing is enough.

Back in 2016, I interviewed 100 women to find out where they were struggling in their self-care.

Every single woman confessed she wasn't exercising enough.

Honestly, it didn't matter how much or what she was doing; she never thought she was doing enough.

But what is enough, and who decides?

What if we change the message from you SHOULD exercise to what COULD you do to move your body, so you feel better mentally and physically?

How does that feel?

Give yourself permission to let go of the should and instead get curious about what would feel good in your body.

What are some secrets for getting yourself to move more?

- Go on a brief walk. Ask a co-worker or friend to join you. Take your dog for a walk.

- Start small - walk for 5 minutes and then walk home. You've just done 10 minutes! Text your BFF and ask them to cheer you on and send you gold stars.

- Try an experiment to collect data. (See Morning Miles example on the next page).

#MorningMiles
Experiment

My history with moving my body is like every other story I have: black/white, hot/cold, on/off.

In my late 40s, I finally had heard enough times from my therapist that binary thinking wasn't doing me any favors, so I decided to try an experiment with movement.

I got curious and wondered what would happen if I walked 20-40 minutes five days a week.

It had been at least two decades since I had moved my body that consistently, and I wanted to see what it would feel like in my decades-older body.

My child was set to attend a summer program a 20-minute walk from our house for 6 weeks. This was my chance!

So I set out every weekday on a walk with my child and then walked 20 more minutes because walking with my kid at the time was slower than molasses on a cold day.

I would take a 3-second video of my feet walking and post it on social media with the hashtag Morning Miles.

Every day I had messages from people cheering me on. Soon others were tagging me with their own walking feet videos, thanking me for getting them outside.

I kept track of my mood and overall feeling of well-being during the experiment.

What I learned is that when I monitor how exercise makes me feel on the inside instead of how it makes me look on the outside.

100% GUILT-FREE SELF-CARE ACTION:

Move your body in a way that feels good. You might want to try:

Asking yourself what did you love doing when you were a kid. What would be fun for you now?

Connecting with a friend with a walk and talk listening to or your favorite podcast or audiobook.

Bouncing on a trampoline or having a kitchen dance party.

SOME QUESTIONS TO WRITE ABOUT IN YOUR SELF-CARE JOURNAL.

What is your exercise story?

What are your childhood experiences with sports or PE class?

What movement feels terrible? What exercise feels like punishment?

Reminder: Stop doing the things that don't feel good. You deserve better.

Make Friends With Your Mind

Our 24-hour news cycle world is noisy.

We are living in stressful times, and we have to take intentional steps to create space in our brains, to cut out the constant chatter, to slow down our pace, and in order to feel less stress.

According to UCLA Medical School, meditation is believed to help relieve stress, lessen depression, lower blood pressure and improve sleep [while boosting] memory, mood, and even social intelligence.

If you want more time, space, and peace: meditate!

The number one reason people tell me they aren't meditating is they aren't good at it.

Just so you know, no one is good at meditating! That is why it is called a *practice*.

Even people who teach meditation are still practicing.

The idea is to sit for 10-15 minutes per day, just watching your breath. The bonus is you also get to watch your thoughts come and go.

A clear mind isn't the goal.

Sitting while watching the breath and thoughts without following every thought is the goal.

During your meditation, your mind will wander. You will think.

You may experience extreme emotions and feelings. You may experience boredom. You may fall asleep.

You may experience an intense urge to get up and do literally anything instead of sitting and watching your breath.

And when you find your attention anywhere except on the breath, with all the gentleness you possess, bring the attention back to the breath. Repeat.

What are some secrets to practicing meditation?

- Set a timer, so you don't have to watch the clock. Or use a meditation app or video.

- Sit in or recline in a comfortable position. Use pillows and blankets to soften your position. Making yourself comfortable helps.

- Go easy on yourself. This sitting doing nothing business is hard. It definitely falls into the simple, but not easy category.

100% GUILT-FREE SELF-CARE ACTION:

Meditate. Sit. Focus on the details of your breath. Notice the air as it comes in through your nose. Notice the rise and fall of your chest and belly.

Use a guided meditation app or video from YouTube.

Or you can simply set a timer for one minute, close your eyes and focus on your breath.

It doesn't have to be fancy to make a difference.

SOME QUESTIONS TO WRITE ABOUT IN YOUR SELF-CARE JOURNAL.

What was your experience with meditation?

What meditation tips were most helpful to you?

What would you do differently next time?

II

The Mental Health Essentials

Taking Care of What Happens in Our Head

What happens in our minds matters. In the not-so-distant past, the body and mind were treated like separate entities.

How early generations dealt with mental health was very different than we do today.

The stigma of mental health care from previous generations is shrinking.

Thankfully going to therapy and working with mental health professionals has much less shame and stigma attached to it than in previous generations.

If you haven't ever explored how therapy can help you, please do. It can change your life in ways you can't yet imagine.

Don't Look Back; You're Not Going That Way.

Not so fast! Adverse Childhood Experiences (ACES): the big T and little T traumas we experienced as children are showing up in our adult lives.

What happened to us as kids has the power to make us sicker and die faster than our peers.

The more traumas experienced, the more long-term health problems that could show up in your adult life.

I know it is difficult to hear, but these experiences don't just go away.

They take up room in your body and cause health problems.

What are some secrets for healing from the past?

- Learn your Adverse Childhood Experiences (ACEs) score.

- Talk to your medical doctor about ACEs and how therapy can help heal ACEs.

- Consistently doing your therapy homework between sessions.

100% GUILT-FREE SELF-CARE ACTION:

Know that ACEs are very common, and you are not alone. Seeking help from a qualified mental health professional is completely normal. More and more people of all kinds are seeking professional help because of the effect mental health can have on our physical health and long-term well-being.

Your doctor can help put you in contact with resources in your community. If you take the ACES test and find out you have a low score, that's fantastic. Therapy can still be beneficial. In therapy, you can get a different perspective on issues in your personal and professional life.

If you learn you have a higher-than-expected score, be gentle with yourself.

SOME QUESTIONS TO WRITE ABOUT IN YOUR SELF-CARE JOURNAL.

What surprised me about ACEs?

What feelings have come up about this new information?

How can you nurture yourself through this experience?

Overwhelm Be Gone

There is a really good chance you feel like you have too much to do and not enough time to do it.

We all have 168 hours per week. Yes, even Beyoncé.

Unless you have the resources to pay other people for their time like Beyoncé, you've got just the 168.

What are some secrets for getting out of overwhelm?

- Do a time audit. Track your time in 15-minute increments.

  Write down everything you did during those 15-minute blocks. Keep track of your time blocks for a few days. You will likely see a pattern of where you are spending your time.

- Say no to things and people that don't add to your life.

- Create white space in your calendar, so you have some breathing room between tasks, activities and projects.

100% GUILT-FREE SELF-CARE ACTION:

Take a phone break. Stay off social media for an hour or a day. Turn off your TV.

SOME QUESTIONS TO WRITE ABOUT IN YOUR SELF-CARE JOURNAL.

What feelings come up when you put your needs and desires first?

What feelings come up and stories do you tell yourself about disappointing people?

In what ways have you benefited from saying yes to everyone and everything so far? What costs have you paid by putting everyone else first?

Be Your Own Cheerleader

Competition and comparison with others sucks the joy out of life.

No one wins and we miss the chance to connect with other people and build strong, supportive communities.

We do better when we feel better, so let's start with cheering on the person we see in the mirror every morning.

What are some secrets to being your own cheerleader?

- Be generous with yourself by believing that you are doing the very best you can in every moment. Some of your moments are going to suck, but it is still your best in that situation.

- Remember, all situations are temporary so you can make amends and do better next time.

- If you catch yourself talking shit about yourself, apologize and give yourself a hug.

100% GUILT-FREE SELF-CARE ACTION:

Practice talking to yourself as if you were a young child.

Look under the behavior and see what it is telling you about the missing need.

For example, if you snapped at your family, instead of beating yourself up and getting stuck there, get curious. Ask yourself what's going on: Are you hungry? Are you tired? Are you needing their help?

Be a feelings detective.

SOME QUESTIONS TO WRITE ABOUT IN YOUR SELF-CARE JOURNAL.

What are some compliments you can give yourself?

What are some things you have done well today?

What is your self-talk like when your needs are being met versus when your needs are not being met?

Look for patterns in your behavior over time. These are clues to what care you need.

When In Doubt, Go Outside

Modern life has many of us inside and on computers for much of our days, much to our detriment.

Science shows nature positively impacts our mood and behavior.

We are physically and mentally healthier when we interact with nature.

Nature helps us by reducing anxiety and stress while increasing attention, creativity and connection with others.

A Japanese study compared urban city walkers and forest walkers. They found the forest walkers had significantly lower heart rates, more relaxation and less stress than the city walkers.

A Finnish study showed that people living in cities who walked for as little as 20 minutes in an urban park versus in the city center showed significantly less stress than the city walkers.

What are some secret ways to get out in nature?

- Investigate green spaces near your home or work so you can have a midday nature walk.

- Look up from your phone when you are outside. Notice how your surroundings change with the seasons.

- Bring nature indoors with plants. Even photos of plants have some of the same benefits.

100% GUILT-FREE SELF-CARE ACTION:

Get outside and take a walk. Notice the sensory details - how does it look, sound, smell, feel?

Bring a friend to a nearby park for a walk.

SOME QUESTIONS TO WRITE ABOUT IN YOUR SELF-CARE JOURNAL.

What outdoor places have you visited in your life that brought you a sense of well-being?

What do those places have in common?

Where would you like to explore in the next year, 5 years, 25 years?

III

The Relationship Essentials

You + Me

VAMPIRES SUCK THE LIFE

Let's face it, after talking with some people, we feel better, like everything in the world is going to be ok.

These people support us; they cheer us on when things are going well and cheer us up when they aren't.

They are available to help us when we need it, and we do the same for them.

We feel connected, understood, heard, and loved.

Then there are the other people. The ones who seem to suck the life out of us.

These are the people who make jokes at our expense, gossip, complain about everything while never coming up with solutions, and try to make us look bad in front of others.

After talking to them, we can feel exhausted, stressed out, guilty, irritated, bored, anxious or depressed.

These folks have a name: energy vampires.

What are some secrets for protecting yourself from energy vampires?

- Pay attention to your body and how it feels when you are with people. Feeling shut down, exhausted, drained? You might have an energy vampire.

- Create an energetic buffer zone. Imagine yourself with some sort of protective shield. Imagine you are suspended in a transparent bubble where nothing can get in. Repeat the mantra: "I'm rubber, you're glue... that bounces off me and sticks to you".

- Limit the time you spend with them. Vampires can only stay in your life if they are invited.

100% GUILT-FREE SELF-CARE ACTION:

Journal it out.

What behaviors drain your energy?

Who are the people who drain your energy?

Assess your friend and family list. Brainstorm ideas of which actions you can take to preserve your energy.

SOME QUESTIONS TO WRITE ABOUT IN YOUR SELF-CARE JOURNAL.

What does setting boundaries look like for you?

What does negativity and gossip feel like in your body?

When in your life have you been an energy vampire in a relationship?

Squad Goals

We go further in life when we have a supportive squad surrounding us.

We get to belong just as we are rather than trying to shape-shift ourselves in order to fit in.

We've already looked at our friend and family list to see who is sucking the life out of us, and now it is time to look at what makes our squad one that is full of trust, respect and love.

What are some secrets for building your squad?

- Be better at boundaries. Setting them, respecting them, & reciprocating them.

- Do what you say you are going to do. Show up.

- Accept responsibility and make amends.

- Keep their secrets secret.

- Believe the best about your people.

100% GUILT-FREE SELF-CARE ACTION:

Reach out in small ways to your most treasured human - send a text saying you were thinking about them - or a meme that made you laugh.

Show up during the hard times and be of service. Listen or hold their hand while they cry. Do not share their stories.

SOME QUESTIONS TO WRITE ABOUT IN YOUR SELF-CARE JOURNAL.

Who in your life do you feel supported by and why?

What are the traits of a good friend and someone you trust?

In what ways are you a good friend to yourself and others?

Being Human Is Hard

Kindness towards ourselves and others makes life a whole lot more pleasant.

It's not common in our culture to show kindness, but we can make the world a more gentle and helpful place by practicing self-compassion.

What are some secrets for practicing self-compassion?

- What we say about ourselves matters. Watch your language. You are a human having a hard time, not the worst person ever. Speak to yourself as if you were someone you love.

- Remember we are all human and that makes us imperfect. Every single one of us has terrible days full of bad decisions and poor behavior. Let's give each other a break so we can do better. Criticism doesn't inspire change.

- Pay attention to when you compare yourself to others or judge people...including yourself. That's a sign it is time to cut people some slack.

100% GUILT-FREE SELF-CARE ACTION:

Practice saying, "I am/they are having a hard time" when things are not going well. Notice how that feels.

Ask yourself what would help you feel better and give yourself permission to do that.

SOME QUESTIONS TO WRITE ABOUT IN YOUR SELF-CARE JOURNAL.

What feelings come up for you when you speak kindly to yourself?

What in your life would change if you were kinder to yourself?

What are the areas in your life where you are most critical of yourself and why do you think that is?

Spirit Essentials

*Being Part of Something
Bigger Than Yourself*

Many people feel connected to something bigger than themselves when they identify as part of a religious community.

Many places of worship do community service projects and help people who are sick and live in under-resourced communities.

For those of us who do not have a connection to a religious community, I want to offer other ways to create connection in your life beyond your immediate family, friends, and neighbors and to create a sense of leaving the world a better place than where you found it.

When we work together, we can make big changes in the world.

Your Contribution Matters

Making the world a more just and equitable place takes collective action.

The first step is to decide what matters to you most and figure out how you can be of service.

Maybe you'd like to help people directly in your own community. This could look like joining a creek cleanup one day in the spring.

You could collect blankets and jackets for families in need and bring them to the shelter.

You could volunteer at your local elementary school to read with students.

You could text bank or write postcards to voters in the midterm elections, or you could run for school board.

Your level of participation will vary depending on the capacity you have in your life right now.

Caring for small children and elderly family members, life transitions like births, deaths, divorces, and new jobs take up a lot of capacity, so be mindful when deciding how you'll get involved.

The good news is that organizations all over the world have been doing this work for decades.

We can ask those who have been doing the work what would be helpful and how we can best utilize our skill set.

What are some secrets for contributing to making the world a better place?

- Remember, no one can do everything, but everyone can do something.

- You don't have to start anything because organizations already have the infrastructure in place.

- Action helps with hopelessness.

100% GUILT-FREE SELF-CARE ACTION:

Join an existing group doing work on an issue you deeply care about.

Volunteer on a political campaign for someone or something you really believe in.

Volunteer to mentor a kid through sports or academics.

SOME QUESTIONS TO WRITE ABOUT IN YOUR SELF-CARE JOURNAL.

What scares you and what inspires you about community activism?

What feelings come up for you when you volunteer your time in your community?

What volunteer jobs did you do as a kid or see your parents do when you were growing up?

Experience Awe

Awe is a feeling of reverence - a deep respect. A spiritual experience is one that can be explained by being created by something bigger than humans.

When I put these two together, I think of the wonders of the natural world.

Some examples that come to mind are:

- The geometry of nature.

- Redwood trees.

- The seasons.

- The ocean.

What are some secrets to creating a feeling of awe?

- Leave your phone inside: go outside and experience it often without distraction. Listen. Look. Feel. Touch. Taste if it is safe.

- Go on a nature hunt: find yellow things, find soft things, find matching things, find symmetrical things, find fluffy things, etc. It may surprise you what you find when you narrow your view.

- Observe close up and also far away: bring a magnifying glass and have a closer look at common objects like leaves and rocks. Lay down and look at the sky. Just watch and wonder.

100% GUILT-FREE SELF-CARE ACTION:

Join an existing group doing work on an issue you deeply care about.

Volunteer on a political campaign for someone or something you really believe in.

Volunteer to mentor a kid through sports or academics.

SOME QUESTIONS TO WRITE ABOUT IN YOUR SELF-CARE JOURNAL.

Would you rather be in the mountains, in the desert, or at the beach?

What draws you to your choice?

What outdoor activities do you enjoy?

What do you wish you knew about the natural world?

Ties That Bind Us Together

People with social ties with like-minded people tend to live longer. Humans are meant to be together.

When we are accepted for who we are - because of our particular brand of weirdness - we belong.

When we find those spaces and places where we can be our most honest selves and be loved and accepted, it feels like magic.

Unlike when we are shapeshifting ourselves in order to fit in.

Your family may be where you belong if you are lucky.

Not everyone's family is where they belong, so you may find your crew somewhere else.

Your like-minded people may be found in a house of worship.

Or you may find your like-minded in a campaign office.

Your like-minded people may be found in a book club.

What are some secrets to finding like-minded people?

- Discover your very niche interests.
    - An example: you like to read. Drill down into more detail. What genre do you enjoy most? You are more likely to find your people, the more specific you can be.

        Contemporary fiction with strong female characters will get you closer than I like fiction.

        Niche book clubs can be found online, and with video conferencing apps, you can join from wherever you live.

- Put your values to work through volunteer hours. Find organizations that work on those issues. Help the causes you care about and meet similarly-minded folks along the way.

- Investigate online groups and meetings in your region. There has never been a better time to connect with like-minded people. With a quick internet search, you can connect with other single women under 40 who love hiking with their dogs.

    If it doesn't exist yet, maybe that's a sign to start the group you'd want to belong to.

100% GUILT-FREE SELF-CARE ACTION:

Let go of guilty pleasures. There is nothing to feel guilty about. You get to like what you like.

Practice self-acceptance around your areas of interest and find people who share your same hobbies. The feeling of belonging is worth the extra effort.

SOME QUESTIONS TO WRITE ABOUT IN YOUR SELF-CARE JOURNAL.

What was a place you have felt safe, loved, and accepted before?

Who are the people you have felt most at home within your life?

What are the most specific hobbies and interests you have at the moment or in the past?

Change What You See and What You See Will Change

How different would the world be if everyone saw the world through other people's experiences?

One way to expand your worldview is to consume media - books, tv shows, comedy specials, movies, educational content, and social media - from people that have different life experiences and backgrounds than yourself.

This gives us a chance to learn from others' experiences.

We get to experience what life is like for other people, and that helps build our empathy.

What are some secrets to finding a new way of looking at the world?

- Be curious and open-minded.

- Listen actively (less talking and much deeper listening) and learn.

- Read a book from a genre you already love from an author from another race, gender identity, region, or part of the world than yourself. Notice similarities and differences.

100% GUILT-FREE SELF-CARE ACTION:

Quickly make a list of your favorite tv shows, movies, and social media accounts.

What do they have in common?

If you are like most, the people in the media you consume look a lot like you.

Watch a TV show, movie or listen to a podcast written by someone with a different background.

SOME QUESTIONS TO WRITE ABOUT IN YOUR SELF-CARE JOURNAL.

What are some similarities you share with authors from around the world?

What are some systematic differences you can find in works of fiction?

What content creators of color do you follow on social media?

Solitude Is Good For Everyone

Throughout history, there has been a lot of talk about introversion and extroversion.

In short, introverts are people who need time alone in order to recharge.

Extroverts are people who get their energy from being with others.

Ambiverts are the folks who straddle the line between introverts and extroverts and likely need a bit of both to recharge.

Like most things in life, it isn't either, and all of us fall on this spectrum and, therefore, can benefit from solitude.

Solitude is the state of being alone and enjoying your own company.

Not to be confused with loneliness - the feeling of isolation.

In other words, we can be content while being alone and we can be isolated while surrounded by others.

What are some secrets to creating solitude?

- Say no to always being busy.

- Schedule alone time in your schedule, just like a meeting with your boss.

- Disconnect from your devices.

100% GUILT-FREE SELF-CARE ACTION:

Start small. Schedule an hour this week to be by yourself, and be sure to disconnect from all of your devices.

Use that time to do nothing or write in your journal, paint, crochet or cook a meal.

SOME QUESTIONS TO WRITE ABOUT IN YOUR SELF-CARE JOURNAL.

What feelings bubble up for you around being alone?

What places and situations in your past have felt peaceful when you were alone?

When in your life have you felt lonely, even when surrounded by people?

Conclusion

You made it!

I hope you have incorporated some of the tips and tools in this book and that you have more time and energy for the people and causes most dear to your heart.

Remember, self-care is less about indulging ourselves with short-term pleasure and more about the actions we take to bring a deeper sense of well-being into our lives now and for our future.

Consistently taking care of our physical, mental, and emotional needs frees up time and builds the energy necessary to create the world we want to live in.

It is my hope that you will return to The Essential Guide to 100% Guilt-Free Self-Care when you need ideas and inspiration for taking care of each aspect of your life.

The world needs your help to create a better place for all of us. I can't wait to see what you do.

ACKNOWLEDGMENTS

Prosper - Thank you for giving me the coaching and encouragement to make this dream a reality.

Thank you to Katie Truman - my right-hand woman. The finisher to my starter. I couldn't do what I do without you.

Thank you to Rosie Molinary and our Flourish year. You help keep me on track and tending to my own care.

Thank you to Catherine. Your generosity and hospitality made the last few years deeply healing.

Thank you to my family and framily. I couldn't love you more if I tried.

FURTHER READING

- *Self-Compassion: The Proven Power of Being Kind to Yourself* by Kristin Neff, PhD

- *FairPlay: A Game-Changing Solution for When You Have too Much to Do (and More Life to Live)* by Eve Rodsky

- *Drop the Ball: Achieving More by Doing Less* by Tiffany Dufu

- *Mindset: The New Psychology of Success* by Carol Dweck

- *Let's Get Physical: How Women Discovered Exercise and Reshaped the World* by Danielle Friedman

- *Better Than Before* by Gretchen Rubin

- *Lazy Doesn't Exist* by Devon Price

- *Set Boundaries, Find Peace: A Guide to Reclaiming Yourself* by Nedra Glover Tawwab

- *The Deepest Well: Healing the Long-Term Effect of Childhood Trauma and Adversity* by Nadine Burke Harris

- *Braving the Wilderness* by Brene Brown

- *Quiet: The Power of Introverts in a World That Can't Stop Talking* by Susan Cain

Articles:

- *Nurtured By Nature: American Psychological Association*
  https://www.apa.org/monitor/2020/04/nurtured-nature

- *Why You Need More Nature In Your Life: Greater Good Science
  Center at UC Berkeley* https://greatergood.berkeley.edu/article/
  item/why_you_need_more_nature_in_your_life

- *Why The World's Best Leaders Want to Meditate On It: Forbes*
  https://www.forbes.com/sites/robasghar/2014/10/29/why-the-
  worlds-best-leaders-want-to-meditate-on-it/

- *Friendships Enrich Your Life and Improve Your Health: Mayo
  Clinic* https://www.mayoclinic.org/healthy-lifestyle/adult-health/
  in-depth/friendships/art-20044860

- *You Probably Need More Alone Time Even If You Are An Extrovert:
  Inc* https://www.inc.com/jessica-stillman/you-probably-need-
  more-alone-time-even-if-youre-an-extrovert.html

- *Lifelong Learning Is Good For Your Health, Your Wallet and Your
  Social Life: Harvard Business Review* https://hbr.org/2017/02/
  lifelong-learning-is-good-for-your-health-your-wallet-and-your-
  social-life

Tami Hackbarth is a Life+Work Coach, the host of the 100% Guilt-Free-Self-Care podcast, and the creator of Deferred Maintenance a group coaching experience.

Clients praise her for her kindness, permission slip giving and her ability to make the impossible seem possible.

Tami Hackbarth
Christina Best Photography

She lives in Sacramento, California with her Old97s record collection, swim goggles, teacher spouse and superhero kid.

Lightning Source UK Ltd.
Milton Keynes UK
UKHW020857220123
415736UK00012B/1907

9 798987 162903